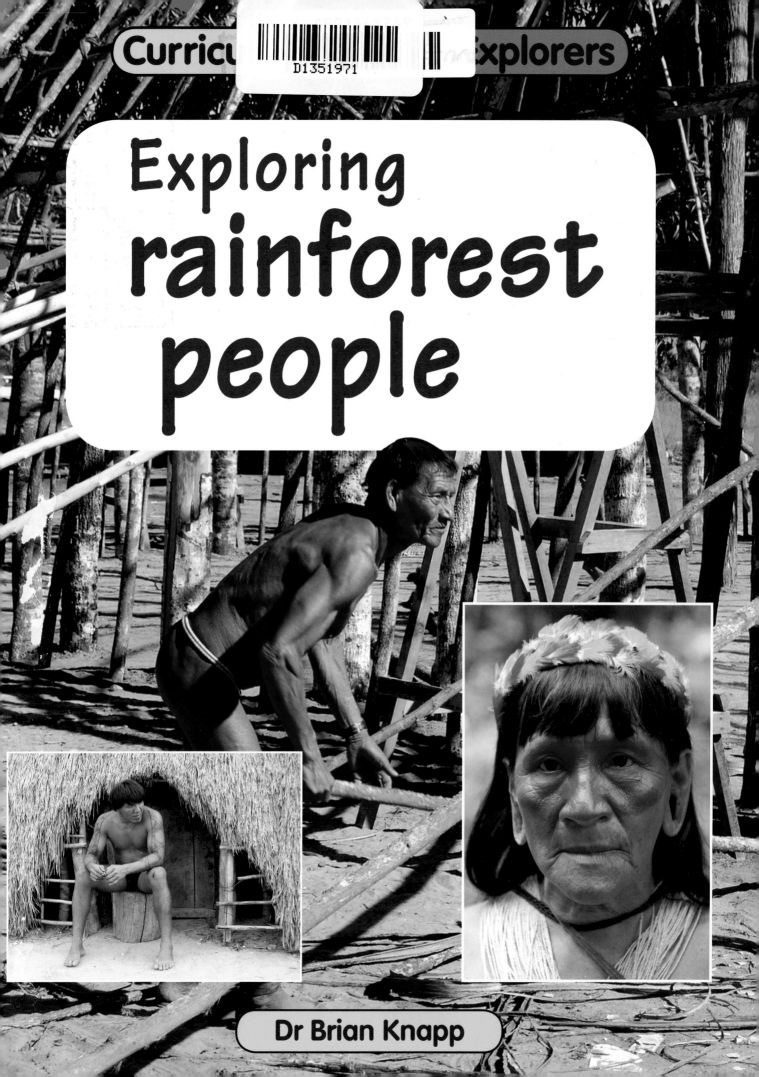

Exploring
rainforest
people

Dr Brian Knapp

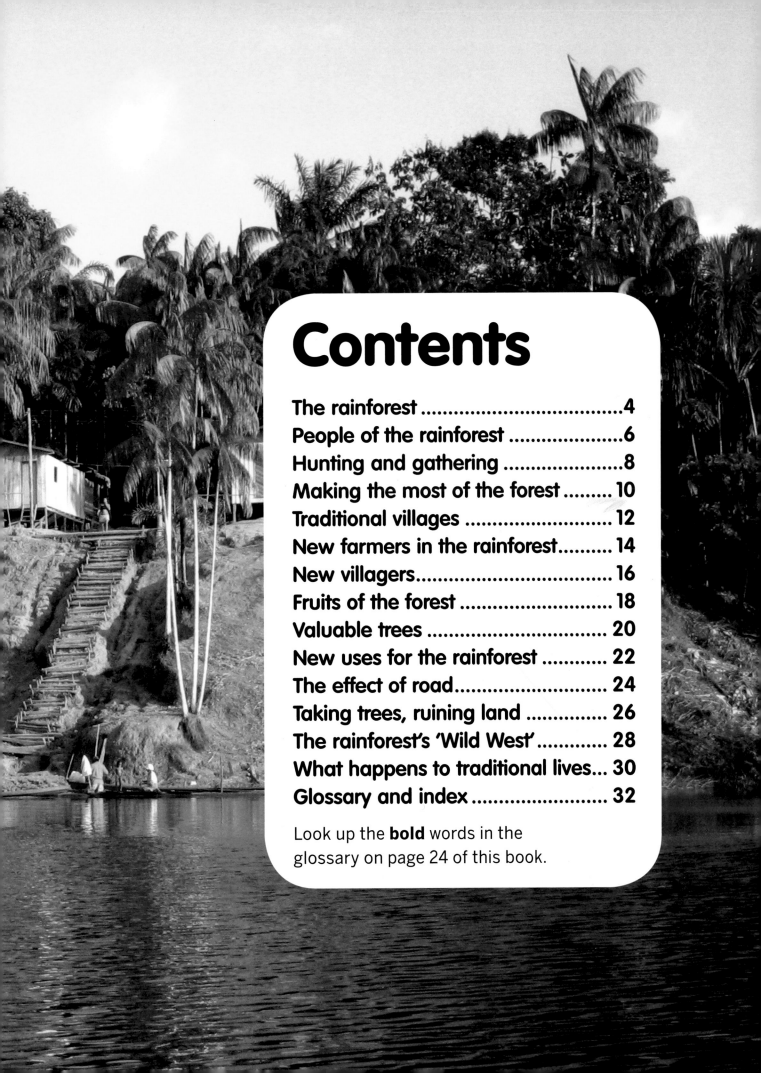

Contents

Look up the **bold** words in the glossary on page 24 of this book.

The rainforest

Here is a natural rainforest. It stretches off without a break to the horizon. It may look all the same, but appearances can be deceiving. It contains many millions of kinds (species) of trees and other plants. In turn, these plants are food and shelter for millions of kinds of animals.

But this is also where some people have lived for hundreds of thousands of years. They have lived in tropical rainforests in Africa, in Papua New Guinea and many Asian islands, and most of all they have lived in the tropical rainforests of the Americas, all the way from southern Mexico (where the Maya civilisation developed) to the vast rainforests of the River Amazon in Brazil.

Until recently, the rainforest has been their world.

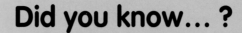

Did you know… ?

- There are more kinds of tree in a square kilometre of tropical rainforest than in the whole of the UK.
- The trees grow well because they recycle their food. The soils are actually very poor.
- The floor of the rainforest of quite shady.
- The trees rise up straight without branches until they reach the sunlight.

Q **Where are the tropical rainforests?**

People of the rainforest

Many years ago a television programme was made whose title was 'Decade of destruction'. It was about the Amazon rainforest in Brazil, and it told the story of how things had changed in just ten years (a decade). The changes were meant to wake up a world that did not realise what was happening. It did, and now many of us are very interested in the rainforests and the living things that make it up. But the destruction still goes on. About one percent more is lost each year. This may not sound much, but it means it will all be gone in a century.

So how is it that the rainforest is being lost so quickly? The answer is, it is an age-old problem. It happened in our country centuries ago, and now we have tiny amounts of forests left. It is all about the growing numbers of people in the world.

The more people there are, the more land they need to feed themselves. But most of the world's people are poor, and the ways they use to feed themselves are often bad for the world as a whole. Then there is the fact that we all want to make our lives more comfortable, and so we want furniture made of nice woods, and pets of pretty colours. And we don't much care how we get them. So we also have ourselves to blame for something that is happening thousands of kilometres away.

Q How much rainforest is being lost each year?

Did you know… ?

- The tropical rainforest is home to more species than the rest of the world put together.
- Many of the foods and medicine we now rely on come from the plants in the rainforest.
- Traditional ways of live depend on people understanding where to look for food and how to catch it or harvest it.
- Many animals, like monkeys, live high in the trees, which is why traditional people developed blowpipes and bow and arrows as a way to reach them.

Hunting and gathering

For countless thousands of years small groups of people (tribes) have gathered fruits, nuts and roots of trees, and hunted wildlife in the trees and in the rivers.

These native peoples have always been experts at feeding themselves, and because they use simple tools they hardly damage the rainforest at all. You can see that on this page.

People select among the great variety of plants and animals in the rainforest. They choose animals that are easy to catch; they find parts of plants that are nourishing, such as bananas, and seed pods containing beans. They also find some things that can make luxuries, such as cacao pods that make chocolate, or honey from wild beehives.

As you can see here, their choices can be surprising, for example, choosing grubs to cook. But grubs are full of nourishment.

But living this way cannot provide food for lots of people. That is because the amount of food that humans can eat is a tiny proportion of what grows.

Banana

Chocolate seed pod

Beans from a seed pod

Grubs are a good so of nourishment

Did you know… ?

• Much of the meat for traditional
  peoples comes from fish in the rivers
  because these are easier to get than
  animals high in the forest canopy.

Cooking fish on an open fire

Making the most of the forest

The rainforest will provide all kinds of things for a good life. People the world over have used the forests for fuel, for food and for building materials.

Here a man is making a frame of a house using the straight trunks of saplings that grow naturally in the rainforest. This reduces the amount of cutting that has to be done, for they only have simple tools. Saplings are also flexible and can be bent to make a curved roof.

The poles are strapped together with vines. The whole house is thatched with palm fronds or grass leaves.

Q Why do they use saplings?

People sleep in hammocks

The roof is thatched

Did you know... ?

- Most traditional rainforest people live in large family groups in big houses.
- In the past, when village groups became too large, part of the village would move away and start a new village.
- Even traditional people can eat food faster than the forest can produce it, so many villages are moved every few years.

Traditional villages

Small collections of huts make a village in the rainforest.

The open area in the middle is where everyone meets to have celebrations.

These people also farm small areas around their village. They are like gardens in size. But only a few tens of metres from the village, the rainforest is still untouched, so you can see that they hardly change the forest at all.

Did you know… ?

- Traditional groups of people have simple needs, so they farm and hunt for as long as it takes to get what they need, then sit back and relax.
- The way of life works well when there are small numbers of people.
- Traditional ways of life need more land to feed people than modern ways of farming, so their way of life is unsuitable when there are large numbers of people in an area (see page 30).

Q Where is the farmland in this picture?

New farmers in the rainforest

People who arrive from outside the rainforest often bring ways of farming with them. But these are not suited to the rainforest.

Here is an example of a poor farmer's hut. Farmers try to survive by keeping chickens and perhaps pigs, as well as growing maize and other crops in areas they have burned off.

To clear the land, the dried forest is burned. It is easy to set fire to it and no tools are needed. Of course, the result is still unsuitable for machinery, so these fields then have to be planted by hand.

The burned trees are turned to ash, and ash is a fertiliser. So for a few years, crops grow well. But when the ash is used up the farmers find the soil is too poor to use any more, so they just abandon it. As a result, the rainforest is destroyed and no one has gained.

Did you know… ?

- Many rainforest governments encouraged poor people to go to the rainforests to try their luck at farming.
- They were not shown how to farm or helped in any way, so most farms failed.

Q Why do many poor farmers fail?

New villagers

All kinds of people make their way to rainforests. They may be poor farmers, or they may be people hoping to set up small shops to sell goods to local people. They may well be working for timber companies, or even working for the many mines that have been set up in these areas.

Did you know… ?

- An area about the size of Wales is being cut down from the world's rainforests each year.
- Many of the rainforest tribes now number just a few thousand people each.

Just like the farmers, these newcomers are not really interested in the forest. They just want to make a living in an ever-more crowded world.

Most of these new villagers live in places that are half village, half farm, as you can see here. Because no one makes much money, they have to grow a little food and rear animals like chickens and pigs, as well as working in shops, cooking in small eateries and so on.

These people have nothing to do with the traditional rainforest peoples. Yet gradually they take over more and more land, so the traditional rainforest peoples have less and less land left.

Fruits of the forest

This picture shows you, literally, 'in a nutshell', the problem of why much rainforest has been destroyed. The rainforest has an enormous variety of plants. Some of them, like this rubber plant, have a liquid in their sap that can be used to make rubber. Here you see how it is tapped and collected.

But in a natural rainforest, there is so much variety that rubber trees are few and far between. So the only way to get more rubber efficiently is to cut down the forest and plant rubber trees in its place. And that is what is in the background.

Did you know… ?

- Many of our most valuable fruits and other products come from tropical rainforest trees.
- When you grow just one kind of plant, the farm is called a plantation. The small pictures show a palm oil plantation. Palm oil comes from the crushed berries and is used in cooking, soap and many other things.

Q Why can't wild rubber trees be used?

Valuable trees

The rainforest has many valuable woods, and huge companies spend their time trying to get them out. The woods are mostly hardwood because that wood is very valuable for making furniture.

Only some trees are suitable, but the rainforest contains a huge variety of trees, so those that are not wanted are often cut down to make logging easier, and then left to rot.

Logs are bulky and heavy, so many are moved out by river. It is possible to grow these valuable trees in plantations. Wood obtained like this is said to come from 'sustainable forests'. If this is done, new areas of rainforest do not have to be harmed.

Did you know… ?

- Trees like teak and mahogany are used in furniture in our homes. Such trees will not grow in other parts of the world.
- It is possible to replant trees like these in the same area, rather than logging out more area. This is called 'sustainable development' and the forests are called 'managed forests".
- You can tell when wood has been bought responsibly by looking at the labels on things you buy.

Q **Why can't most trees be used?**

New uses for the rainforest

There is no doubt that, if you are to find food for many people, you must replace some forest with fields.

One of the biggest yields of food in a rainforest area is by growing rice. The small picture shows rice paddy fields. Rice is a native to swamps of hot, wet areas, and so grows well in former rainforest land.

Much of the rainforest of Asia has been replaced by rice fields, and now you might not even recognise it as an area that was once rainforest.

Another thing that can be tried is to plant grass and allow cattle to graze among the charred stumps. This works for a few years, too, but in the end the grass uses up all the ash and stops growing.

Did you know… ?

- There are two kinds of rice: paddy rice and dry rice. Paddy rice grows naturally in swamps, which is why the fields are kept waterlogged.
- Rice can support thousands of time more people than a rainforest.
- Cattle grazing is a very inefficient way of using land.
- These new kinds of farming will only work if fertilisers are used, so they tend to be more suitable for farmers who have large areas of land, and the money to buy fertiliser. Small farmers with little money would find this much harder.

Q Which can support more people: rice or cattle?

The effect of roads

Start by looking at the hill in the background. It is still covered with rainforest.

This is Asia, and the government has built a road into the forest land. It runs along the ridge. Farmers have poured into this area to replace forest with fields.

All kinds of crops are being grown here because the road allows the crops to be taken easily to market.

But the slopes are very steep and so landslides are common, and soil is often washed away during big storms.

Did you know... ?

- Asia has very little rainforest left because it has many people, and mostly forest been changed to farmland.
- The places with the largest rainforest remaining are in the Congo Basin of Africa and the Amazon of Brazil
- The Amazon is at threat because the country is developing fast and its population is growing quickly.

Q Why can people get their crops to market easily?

Taking trees, ruining land

Large areas of rainforest make their own weather. They give off (transpire) huge amounts of water through their leaves. This moisture rises in the warm air, makes clouds which then rain and give water to the soil.

So when people cut down trees, either for the wood or to grow crops, they make drought more likely. But most of the rain still comes in on the winds, and when it falls, it comes down like cloudbursts. The rainforest leaves take up the shock of these heavy raindrops, while the tree roots loosen up the soil and hold it together, so that the rain will seep into the ground.

But when the trees are taken away, the rain falls on bare soil and washes it away. The soil is not held together by tree roots, so it slips away, making landslides. The rain does not seep in, but runs over the surface, getting into rivers and making floods.

Look at how ruined this land in Costa Rica has become.

Q Why are landslides more common?

Did you know... ?

- Flooding has become a much more serious problem since trees were cut down. Far more people lose their lives in the tropics from floods and landslides that in the past.
- When land is abandoned, it is difficult for natural trees to regrow because the soil has been washed away. So the land is ruined for everything.

The rainforest's 'Wild West'

You have probably heard of the American Wild West. It was a frontier region in the nineteenth century, where people arrived to claim land (from the Indians) to farm and to take minerals like gold from the rocks.

Today, many of the world's 'Wild West' areas are in rainforests. The rocks have gold, the land has valuable trees, and it seems to some to be a land that is 'wasted' because it is not being used (except by the traditional peoples, of course).

There is very little control on what newcomers do in some of these areas. Most of the people who move in to rainforests are poor. They build towns of shacks. In South America these are called favelas. No one puts in sewage plants or provides clean water. The river in this picture is a grey colour because the raw sewage in it has killed off all life.

Such changes are a threat to all rainforests.

Did you know... ?

- Many rainforest towns are very remote, so it is expensive to put in new services like sewers.
- Countries with rainforests often cannot afford to put in services.
- Some people make a lot of money by spending as little on services and help for the poor as possible.

Q Why is there no fish in rivers close to some rainforest towns and cities?

What happens to traditional lives?

As you have seen, there are many people who want to come to the rainforest. Some just want to make money easily, others come because they are poor and want a better life.

So what happens to the way of life of the traditional people? Most have already lost their lands. They have been resettled in areas which are not 'in the way' of progress.

A few, like the Kayapo tribe have been 'protected'.

The Kayapo tribe lives in the Amazon Rainforest in several scattered villages containing one hundred to one thousand people. They need 11 million ha of land to survive in a traditional way, even though there are just nine thousand of them.

Some tribal people are of interest to tourists. But when tourists come, they change the way of these people forever. So the chances of people being able to keep a traditional way of life in the future are almost nonexistent.

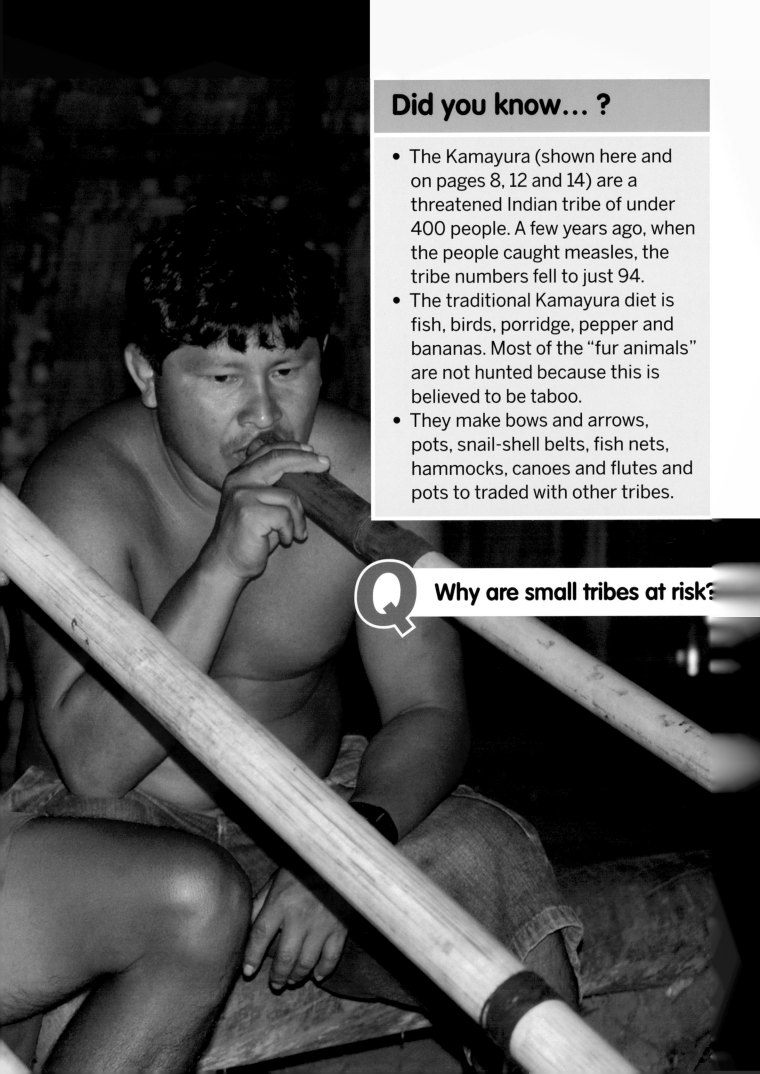

The Kamayura (shown here and on pages 8, 12 and 14)

Did you know… ?

- The Kamayura (shown here and on pages 8, 12 and 14) are a threatened Indian tribe of under 400 people. A few years ago, when the people caught measles, the tribe numbers fell to just 94.
- The traditional Kamayura diet is fish, birds, porridge, pepper and bananas. Most of the "fur animals" are not hunted because this is believed to be taboo.
- They make bows and arrows, pots, snail-shell belts, fish nets, hammocks, canoes and flutes and pots to traded with other tribes.

Q Why are small tribes at risk?

Glossary

blowpipe

A long natural pipe, for example, made out of bamboo, that can be used to shoot a dart simply by blowing sharply at one end.

fertiliser

A material used to give extra nourishment to plants

frontier region

A region which is not well developed

landslide

A sudden movement of large amounts of soil and rock down a hillside

logging

To cut down trees on a large scale

plunder

To take away without thought of the result in the future

sap

The natural liquid inside a plant

sapling

A very young tree plant

taboo

Something that people have agreed they would not do

thatched

A roof made of reeds and grasses

Index

Curriculum Visions

Curriculum Visions Explorers
This series provides straightforward introductions to key worlds and ideas.

You might also be interested in
Our *Dig Deeper* book, Rainforest life, and others such as Exploring the endangered rainforest.

www.CurriculumVisions.com

(Subscription required)

© Atlantic Europe Publishing 2014

The right of Brian Knapp to be identified as the author of this work has been asserted by him in accordance with the Copyright, Designs and Patents Act 1988.

Author
Brian Knapp, BSc, PhD

Senior Designer
Adele Humphries, BA, PGCE

Editors
Gillian Gatehouse
Emily Pulsford, BA

Designed and produced by
Atlantic Europe Publishing

Printed in China by
WKT Company Ltd

**Exploring rainforest people
– Curriculum Visions**
A CIP record for this book is available from the British Library.

Paperback ISBN 978 1 78278 078 6

Picture credits
All photographs are from the Earthscape and ShutterStock Picture Libraries.

This product is manufactured from sustainable managed forests. For every tree cut down at least one more is planted.